Patrick Martin King

Verses

Patrick Martin King

Verses

ISBN/EAN: 9783744651998

Printed in Europe, USA, Canada, Australia, Japan

Cover: Foto ©Thomas Meinert / pixelio.de

More available books at **www.hansebooks.com**

VERSES

BY

PATRICK MARTIN KING

SAN FRANCISCO

1890

PREFACE.

Herewith are printed, for some friends, a few of the trifles which, from time to time, I have sent to the newspapers, with others that have not yet appeared in print. To them are added those that I have sent to Her Gracious and Imperial Majesty, The Queen of England.

That my poor thoughts are not more artistically sent forth is cause for regret, but that they are honest, that they come from the heart, I trust none will doubt. "*Haud facile emergunt quorum virtutibus obstat res angusta domi*" is a truism recognized to-day as fully by every man having any pretensions to literary attainments, as it was by him from whom I quote.

With these few remarks I launch my little skiff and hope that she may bring "good luck" to all she may reach.

>Frail nautilus, I fling thee
>On ocean smooth and clear.
>May gentle zephyrs wing thee
>To all that I hold dear.

P. M. K.

SAN FRANCISCO, May, 1890.

CONTENTS.

	Page.
PREFACE TO THE POEMS	3
CONTENTS	5
A CALIFORNIA FERN-LEAF	9
A WISH	12
TWO LIPS AND ROSES	14
TO THE SOUL	16
NATURE'S NOBLEMAN	18
A VALENTINE	20
THE CHRISTIAN POET	23
THE GENIAL POET	25
NATURE'S POET	27
SONG: *Cleveland and Thurman*	31
A THANKSGIVING ODE	35
INDEPENDENCE DAY	38
A REGRET	42
A REMEMBRANCE	45
RETRO SATANAS	47

ONLY A POET	50
PARK LYRICS:	
Irish Eyes	53
Bright Chataine	55
Twilight — Sunlight — Flowers — Women	57
A SKETCH: *The Real and the Ideal*	59
A BIRTHDAY WISH	61
TO HER	62
A HEALTH TO HER	64
TO MESDAMES S—— AND T——	66
A STAVE FOR IRELAND	68
AN ODE OF THANKSGIVING	70
A MONODY	72
AN INTROSPECTIVE MUSING	74
TO "A" (in reply to her request)	77
LE JOUR DE L'AN	80
PEN PORTRAITS:	
Archbishop Riordan	84
Vicar-General Father Prendergast	84
The Chancellor, Father Montgomery	85
A SERENADE	86
HEALTH TO SUE	88

BACCHANALIAN	91
A RECOLLECTION OF THE YOSEMITE	92
A VALENTINE	94
MUSING	97
A CHRISTMAS CAROL	99
A PARK CAROL	101
NOTES TO IRISH RECOLLECTIONS	103
IRISH RECOLLECTIONS:	
Martin Toole	105
Father James	108

A CALIFORNIA FERN-LEAF:

CULLED FOR THE QUEEN.

DEDICATED TO
The Prince of Wales.

A health to England's Empress-Queen —
The best, the truest, that has been
Since monarchy first graced the scene —
    From this fair land is sent; —
This land that now would be her own,
Had George the Third when on the throne
But listened to his people's tone,
    And grandly to it bent.

Live, Mistress fair of lands and seas
In torrid zones and climes that freeze,
Greater than ever Rome in these —
    Thou art thy nation's choice;

And on this day in every land,
On every sea, on every strand
Where English-speaking people band,
    They hail thee with glad voice.

And I have seen thee years ago,
When in my veins youth's blood did flow,
Not then as now so calmly slow —
    It was in my sad sireland ;—
The brightest jewel in thy crown,
Above the "Kohinoor's" renown,
Oh! smile on her and never frown,
    She is thine own, brave Ireland.

And if I now a fancy weave,
'T is not to flatter or deceive,
Nor would I say aught that might grieve
    On this thy natal day;
But I have found in other times
That good has come from humble rhymes,
Though inartistic be the chimes,
    And so, accept my lay.

O Queen, long may you live to see
That justice best controls the free,
And in it power shall ever be
    To stamp out hate and treason;
But, Empress great, with justice blend
Mercy to all, and so defend
Your own good name unto the end
    By linking love with reason.

And when the earthly crown is gone,
Descending to thy loyal son,
The Sovereign Lord shall say "Well done";
    And in the realms above
Give thee a crown that cannot die,—
A crown beyond the azure sky
That all destruction shall defy,
    In token of His love.

SAN FRANCISCO, CALIFORNIA,
    MAY 24, 1889. (The Queen's Birthday.)

A WISH:

LINES ON THE MARRIAGE OF THE PRINCESS LOUISE.

Ring out, ye joy bells, ring,
And to this Princess sing
The homage that ye bring
    With loud and joyous voice.
She of the regal line,
Victoria, is thine;
In her thy virtues shine—
    Let Englishmen rejoice.

Rejoice, and to Him pray
That His protection may
To her extend alway
    A kind almighty friend;
That her career be bright,
She guided by His light,
And walking in His sight,—
    With Fife's love to defend.

Strew flowers 'neath her feet;
Let cheers her presence meet;
With language loud yet sweet
    Be loyalty expressed.
This day let anthems rise
Melodious to the skies;
With feeling that ne'er dies
    Be sympathy confessed.

O, may her days be long,
While history and song
The Good and True among
    Her name shall wreathe.
This from a distant clime,
With harp ill kept in time,
But in well meaning chime,—
    The wish I breathe.

TWO LIPS AND ROSES:

A RECOLLECTION.

Once 'neath Cathedral dome,
Not Peter's shrine in Rome
But Mary's here at home,
    I saw a gentle girl
With roses in her hand
That followed love's command,
Nor could the spell withstand
    Of sweetening this pearl.

The girl! When she looked down
The roses couldn't frown,
But held their leaves, though brown,
    As craving for Love's sips;
The brown leaves turned to green
More verdant in love's sheen
Than they had ever been,
    While drinking from her lips.

Ah, me! that day how I
Would give my life and die
And forfeit earth and sky,
    Could I but be that rose!
For one fond hour to lie
Upon her breast and sigh
Out life in love, then die,—
    Such death is sweet repose.

SAN FRANCISCO,
    December 28, 1889.

TO THE SOUL.

Spirit of mine, look on!
Thou'rt surely best alone,
Thy destiny undone,
   Than with the vulgar throng.
If lust for many things
Possession some time brings,
Remorse yet subtly stings—
   God placed thee on thy throne.

Sorrow may stress and try,
Fondest of hopes may die,
Love may but leave a sigh,
   Yet kills not, though it mars.
Sorrow is helpless ire,
Ambition, vain desire,
Love, a malingering fire—
   Over the clouds are stars.

Then, O my soul, we'd crave
Of Him, who to us gave
The thoughts the heart to lave
   To upward look for ever;
And, if it be, that now
Grief must weigh down the brow,
We'll hold on to the plow,
   And leave the furrow—never.

NATURE'S NOBLEMAN:

SUGGESTED ON READING OF THE DUKE'S REFUSAL OF THE ROYAL DOWRY.

O lordly Fife, well done,
Thou hast Wales' Princess won,
And gold thou touchest none,
    All honor unto thee.
Rejecting "Royal Grants,"
Accepting but love's thanks,
You elevate the ranks
    Of modern chivalry.

True chip, from old Macduff,
Thou criest, "Hold, enough,
We are not of the stuff
    That pawns the heart for gold,
Though living in this age
Of mercenary rage
Our honor you must gauge
    As in the days of old."

Thus, I, in dreamy rhyme
Of past and present time,
Hail thee on height sublime,
    Front in manhood's peerage;
And, as my lot is cast
With those before the mast,
I offer homage last
    Coming from the steerage.

SAN FRANCISCO,
    October 5, 1889.

A VALENTINE.

Away from Kentucky's green mountains,
  Away from its bright skies of blue,
Away from its dancing clear fountains
  I hasten to gaze upon you!

Those landscapes so fair are behind me!
  Now torrents and gorges before—
I care not. All things but remind me
  To hasten and see you once more.

I am come. Do not turn you so coldly,
  Nor scorn my poor frivolous lay;
It may be "the last" though thus boldly
  I hail you on Valentine's Day!

I hail you, my dearest, so youthful;
  I hail the fresh bloom on your cheek;
I hail you in verse that is truthful;
  In words now forbidden to speak.

And you, O Saint Valentine clever,
  I hail and pay homage, your Grace;
I'll pray at your altar forever,
  For through you I look in her face.

Let the day and occasion excuse me,
  And the weary long many a mile
I have traveled—you cannot refuse me
  What I'd barter my soul for—one smile.

And that smile though to cold paper given,
  And that paper and I far apart;
Though from you and from heaven I'm riven
  That smile shall come on to my heart.

And if I would ask one more favor—
  How cheap with my life-blood 'twere bought—
One smile you will give to this paper,
  And keep for the writer—one thought.

And that thought when in moments of gladness
  You list to the voices of love,

Shall come over his soul in its sadness,
  As dew comes from heaven above.

That smile and that thought linked together,
  Concession from beauty to pain,
Will tell him in fair or foul weather
  His life has not all been in vain.

THE CHRISTIAN POET.

With his own soul alone he talks
In crowded streets or quiet walks,
Nor careth for the many balks
    That may beset his ways;
For trusting in his God on high—
The God of earth and sea and sky
Who unto him is ever nigh—
    He gives his thoughts in lays.

In lays betimes of dreamy mood
All written for the people's good,
And by them little understood
    Whilst with them here he stays;
But when He shall His servant call
To leave the scene of man's first fall
Nor further drain life's bitter gall
    Then they may read his lays.

And, yet perchance, it may come out
They know not what they are about
When echoing forth their rabble shout :
    "We'll give him now a stone!"
For when the noble man is dead
And needs no more his daily bread ;
They'll place a marble o'er his head
    And think they thus atone.

THE GENIAL POET.

He cares not for the titled "Noddy,"
He scoffs and scorns the upstart "Shoddy,"
Though smilingly he'll try a toddy,
    As every good man may;
And with true men from night 'til morn
He'll sip the juice of grape or corn,
And smoke away all thought forlorn
    In true Bohemian way.

And then he's glad to hear you talk
In rushing ride or sober walk,
And his good jokes you cannot balk
    For he will have his say;
And when in humor he has got
He'll give you back each well-bred shot
With not a touch of vulgar "rot"
    Until the break of day.

And thus his days and nights along
He'd spend in wit and wine and song
His tried and trusty friends among —
    Young though they be or mellow;
And when at last his soul has fled
To seek the regions of the dead,
Of him it may be truly said,
    He wasn't a bad fellow.

NATURE'S POET.

In Fancy's land he lives and loves,
And 'midst her fields he freely roves
With flowers of thought culled from her groves
    Which he would share with you;
Nor sect, nor creed he will revere
On this or any other sphere,
At home, abroad or anywhere
    Save what is good and true.

Your jargon oft he will forsake
"For moonbeams glassed upon the lake,"
Or sunlight glinting through the brake
    As it may suit his whim;
"His words are idle — oft times mad,"
If in his moods he's aught but sad —
Say on! If it but makes you glad
    It is the same to him.

He flies from you—he hates you not,
Nor are your sorrows e'er forgot,
Though seeming happy be your lot
    He knows you are not so;
He knows that in each human breast
There is a foe to human rest—
Call it you may the worst, or best—
    The heritage of woe.

Then he will leave you oft awhile
To bask in Nature's bonnie smile,
Adown life drifting mile on mile
    Led onward by her voice.
Anon he hears the twittering birds—
To his true soul, melodious words,
All touching transcendental chords—
    Nor with dull selfish choice.

He lists the murmuring of brooks;
The stones he treads to him are books;
The flowers that bloom in brakes or nooks
    Are mirror'd in his soul.

He looks up to the stars on high,
Illumining night's velvet sky,—
To whom his spirit would draw nigh
    Thought-free, from Pole to Pole.

He views the hoary mountains old
Now bleak and gray and barren cold,
But soon all framed in burnished gold
    As day begins to die,—
When Sun-god mad with wrath and ire
Leaves fading world to darkness dire,
And steeps the western marge in fire,—
    In roseate tints the sky.

He wanders on—each flower he sees,
Each tiny shoot—the aged trees,
And tenderly with all of these
    He would communion hold.
He'd ask of them, when he was young,
If from their parentage he sprung;
If he like them first had no tongue
    If he was e'er so cold.

Of streams' soft voice or oceans' roar
He'd ask what of his state before,
Or what may be when nevermore
    His eyes look on this scene.
He longs and thirsts for knowledge all
From the "beginning" to the "fall,"
And since. But to his earnest call
    No answer yet has been.

He stands upon earth's vernal sod,
Yet scorns the beaten paths to plod;
He'd tread those heights that ne'er were trod
    In all the ages long.
His spirit droops, his reason reels,
As o'er his soul the dire thought steals
That feeling all, he naught reveals,
    And leaves unsung his song.

A CAMPAIGN SONG.

DEDICATED TO

Mrs. Cleveland

(WIFE OF THE PRESIDENT.)

Men of our great and glorious land,
Men who've come here from foreign strand,
Now muster in fraternal band
    For Cleveland and for Thurman;
For they are battling for the right,
And waging here the people's fight;
Therefore, come on in all your might
    For Cleveland and for Thurman!

CHORUS.

Men who have loved your country so,
Men who will shout "Chinese must go,"
Now let your votes right loyal flow
    For Cleveland and for Thurman;

For they will sure your country purge,
And drive right out the heathen scourge;
Therefore, let each the other urge
    For Cleveland and for Thurman!

                              CHORUS.

Men crushed to earth with taxes high,
Men holding thoughts not born to die,
Now let your voices reach yon sky
    For Cleveland and for Thurman;
For they this tariff so accurst,
Will in all equity adjust;
Therefore, freemen, march on you must
    For Cleveland and for Thurman!

                              CHORUS.

Men who will think and men who toil,
Men of the workshop and the soil,
Go straight ahead—there's no recoil—
    For Cleveland and for Thurman;

For they will sure your needs supply,
And foreign influence defy;
Therefore, go forward in full cry
    For Cleveland and for Thurman!

                                    Chorus.

Men oft by Grant to victory led,
Men who with Lee have fought and bled,
Now march, this time, in tranquil tread
    For Cleveland and for Thurman;
They ne'er in thought and act will cease,
Nor will their efforts e'er decrease,
Till Gray and Blue be blent in peace
    For Cleveland and for Thurman!

                                    Chorus.

Men free and brave from every strand,
Now voters here in freedom's land,
With Right and Justice take your stand
    For Cleveland and for Thurman;

And be but loyal each true son,
The fight's your own—the battle's won,
And we shall land in Washington
    For Cleveland and for Thurman!

Chorus.

We'll march right on for Cleveland and for Thurman,
We'll march right on nor loiter by the way,
We'll march right on for Cleveland and for Thurman,
We'll march right on, we're ready for the fray!

A THANKSGIVING ODE.

DEDICATED TO

Hon. Thos. F. Bayard,

Sans peur et sans reproche.

We thank you, Cleveland, for this call
To render our Thanksgivings all,
For many blessings, great and small,
    By which we are surrounded.
And all you Deities on high,
Who wield your sceptres in the sky,
To you just now we'd fain draw nigh
    In faith, howe'er unfounded.

And yet amidst your varied crew
Of whimsical, or false, or true,
Amidst your lot I choose but two—
    Ceres and jolly Bacchus;

For sure, without their timely aid
I must confess I am afraid,
And honestly it must be said
    Venus would not attack us.

And without Venus what were earth!
A wretched, soulless, barren berth,
Of hope and life and joy the dearth—
    Of sons and wife and pater,
No more we'd find down here below;
Our age a blank where'er we'd go,
Weeds tempest-tossed all to and fro,
    Without thee, Venus Mater.

But since we have you, Venus, dear,
With Ceres and with Bacchus near,
That 't is our duty is quite clear
    To live whilst life is living;
And so I fill the wine-cup high,
And drink to those 'throned in the sky,
And unto Cleveland, far more nigh,
    In thanks for his "Thanksgiving."

Then let us here the goblet fill,
And pledge to all men of good will
Whose hearts to virtue ever thrill
    With constancy full blended ;
And with them I include the true,
The ever-faithful gallant crew
That manned the ship well sailed by you,
    Whose voyage now is ended.

And still once more the cup I'll drain,
Unto you, Cleveland. Yes, again,
And this, for aye, is my refrain,
    Truth, Loyalty and Honor ;
And confusion to all those
False-hearted knaves, not straight-out foes,
Who have prolonged a nation's woes
    By battening upon her.

INDEPENDENCE DAY:

LINES SUGGESTED BY READING A PESSIMISTIC ARTICLE IN A LOCAL HEBDOMADAL.

Come, muse of mine, in Freedom's cause
We'll touch the lyre, nor fear the laws
Of pedagogues in our see-saws
    As we may canter on;
We sing not here of Marathon,
Of wars by Greeks or Persians won,
Nor shall we bask in Roman sun—
    They're past—though never gone.

This day we choose a modern theme—
That to our souls would almost seem
Fulfilment of the poet's dream—
    Nor sigh for aught beside;

We sing the present, our own times,
Albeit in unworthy rhymes,
And mayhap in discordant chimes
    Which critics may deride.

We sing of our own race and kin;
Of those of old who did begin
A manly war on thraldom's sin;
    To those who in their might
Still later asked and were refused,
And asked again and were ill-used;
Then, nobly fought and blood diffused
    And conquered for the right.

We hail this English-speaking man
Whose fight for Freedom once began
With Magna Charta, and thence ran
    O'er every sea and strand,
Uplifting man wherever found
From slavery, however bound,
His course the entire world around
    To settle in this land.

O wholesome land of liberty!
True glowing sprout from olden tree—
Still may thy mission onward be
    For Truth to ever fight;
And with thy parent hand in hand
On every sea, on every strand,
United be in filial band
    For Freedom and for Right.

And on that day this world shall see
Man's universal jubilee,
With watchword, ever, "Liberty!"—
    From every port and bay;
When Flag of England is combined
With Stars and Stripes upon the wind—
Then, despots shall a lesson find,
    Nor dare to court the fray.

So, long live "Independence Day"
The griefs of Freedom to allay,
And in men's thought remain alway
    Unto far distant time.

Thus sixty millions this day cry
Whilst rockets screech unto the sky,
As cannons thunder far and nigh,
    And with them goes my rhyme.

SAN FRANCISCO, CALIFORNIA,
    July 4, 1889. (Independence Day.)

A REGRET.

"Farewell to the White House," cried Cleveland, its master,
Just after the recent election disaster.
"Farewell, to the dreams of advancing in glory
This great country's fame and my own name in story!
Farewell to the hopes, to the joys, and some tears
That I've borne so calmly now over four years!
Farewell, you tired days and you days all too pleasant!
Farewell to the White House! I say for the present.
Farewell to them all! I'm still loyal and true
And can bid all good-bye to live now for you."

"Farewell to the White House!" sighed the fairest of women
Whose beauty e'er thralled the hearts of all freemen.

"Farewell!" she sighs sadly, though outwardly
    seeming
To this change unconscious, she's inwardly
    dreaming.
Her dreams are the dreams of the Pure and the
    Truthful,
The Cultured, the Well-bred, the Winsome and
    Youthful.

"Farewell to the White House!" cried Bayard,
    a man
Without fear or reproach or dishonest plan.
"I have done my duty 'fore God and true men;
And if I've done wrong I would do it again.
I've loved this great country, its land and its sea,
And no party e'er served it less selfish than we.
Whate'er may betide me let fate not o'erwhelm,
I'm ready when called to again take the helm.
If rough days I've had, I have also had pleasant;
And say with my chieftain, "Farewell for the
    present!"

"Farewell to the White House!" cry the loyal and true
That well sailed the ship with her captain all through;—
And I at this distance say, "Fare-*well* to those
And ill may it fare to all dishonest foes!"

A REMEMBRANCE.

I think of thee as morning breaks
   To chase the mist of night,
And vapors rise from distant lakes
   To the Sun's all-cheering light.

I think of thee as noontime warm
   Comes o'er the earth so still,
And zephyrs dance in cooling charm
   On crests of highest hill.

I think of thee as evening calm
   Mourns for the dying day,
And flowers breathe a fragrant balm,
   For, oh, they cannot stay.

I think of thee as twilight hour
   Steals o'er us from above,
And human hearts have lost their power
   In longing thirst of love.

I think of thee as night goes on—
　　When stars above are brightest,
But I must join the inane throng
　　With heart as of the lightest.

I think of thee as midnight hour
　　Forsakes the day that's gone,
And nought is heard in hall or tower
　　Save crannying winds alone.

I think of thee the next day then
　　As on the day before,
And long for happy future when
　　I'll clasp thy hand once more.

RETRO SATANAS.

Dreams of my boyhood! Why rise you just now
With grief in my heart and care on my brow?
Back, back to your caves! Your wings closely
　　　furled;
For know you the fact we are now in the world!
Away with your notions of Cæsar and Brutus,
There is but one god here, and his name is
　　　Plutus;—
That great healer, he, of all earthly ills,
They melt into air when he wipes out your bills!

Then, Master of Riches, 't is you I'll adore,
When trouble assails me 't is you I'll implore.
If sickness o'ertakes me, the doctor you'll pay,
And if I court honors—why, you'll pave the
　　　way;
And that one ambition, all others above,
You can purchase for me—a true woman's love!

Foul fiend, thou liest! Do all that you can
With fallen, degraded, irresolute man;
But know you, false tempter, there's one thing
    at least
In this wretched age that is not of the beast;
It is this priceless jewel from heaven above
Still pure and unsullied — a good woman's love.

Then dreams of my boyhood, of innocent youth,
Let us dream as of yore of the Right and the
    Truth!
Let us rock on the ocean, and sail on the lake,
Let us climb the high mountain, and rest in the
    brake;
Let us bask in the sunshine, and cool in the
    shade,
Let us drink in the beauties of woodland and
    glade!
Let us look to the stars, and list to the streams,
Let us roam in the moonlight and follow its
    beams;

Let us, O God, in Thy mercy, gaze high,
Let us turn from the earth and look to the sky;
Let us fly from this world, with its pitfalls, its sin,
Let us dream the old dreams, our own world within!

ONLY A POET.

"Only a poet"—O, that night so rare!
    The stars were glistening in God's dome o'erhead,
And I stood with the girl that I loved there,
    Listening to what the trembling ocean said.

"Only a poet"—And the soft winds blow,
    And I am lying loving at her feet,
Her breathings reach me quick and sweet and low,
    And loose my soul I dare not—nor retreat.

"Only a poet"—Yet who fain would sing
    His song of Truth and Hope and Light and Love;
Who far would soar on sweep of angels' wing,
    Nor stop until he reached God's throne above.

"Only a poet"—With a poet's soul,
    And love for all things holy, pure and bright ;
  Oft sunk in reverie past will's control,
    He cannot speak a single thought to-night.

"Only a poet"— With the poet's scorn
    For aught that vile or vulgar is or low ;
  Who yet can weep with suffering gently born
    And laugh at tinsel shine on shoddy's brow.

"Only a poet"— Bowed down to earth
    Beneath the weight of man's primeval curse ;
  Though his face be fanned with heaven's own breath,
    'Tis hell he carries in his empty purse.

"Only a poet"— Glorious, welcome taunt
    So oft applied by scorners empty-brained,
  Whose only wealth, whose single blatant vaunt
    Is but the filthy lucre they have gained.

"Only a poet"—Wishing that he were,
    For then he'd sing you songs both clear and bright—
Songs that would banish far both grief and care,
    And lift the soul to God and Truth and Right.

"Only a poet"—'T was whispered soft,
    As I knelt bewitched and loth to go,
With zephyrs sighing tremulous and oft
    And moonbeams kissing silvery waves below.

"Only a poet"—And who then is this—
    Booby, Noodle—or perhaps some other
Whose presence mars this hour of double bliss?
    'T is neither one—confound it—'t is her brother.

PARK LYRICS.

Irish Eyes.

I dream, I dream, of Irish eyes
That gazed in mine with shy surprise;
Two Irish eyes of honest gray—
Soft as a soft autumnal day.

They are not gray! I see them blue—
Those windows to a heart so true.

I see them now! They are jet black
As thunder cloud upon the wrack,
Ere to the lightning it gives birth
And tearful meltings fall to earth.

Slanderer, avaunt! They are not jet
But of the loveliest violet—
Those long-loved, long-lost violet eyes
That looked in mine with glad surprise.

I've quaffed Love's draught on many a strand,
'Neath many a sky, in many a land;
I've seen fair dames on many a shore
Beautiful as the loved of yore;
I've seen them, and I see them now
With culture stamped on classic brow
As musing thus, their looks I mark
Whilst strolling in your "Golden Park."

Yes, many a fair one I descry
With instep arched and roguish eye,
And many a Hebe. Sometimes a Juno,
Surpassed in grace by none that you know,
Whose handsome hands, whose shapely feet
The backward flowers spring to meet.

There are grand dames beneath these skies—
But, ah! I dream of Irish eyes.

Bright Chataine.

Last week we sang of Irish eyes
Which we had seen 'neath murky skies
In that old land—the land of Pat,
Of Priests, Coercion, and all that.

To-day we sing a brighter theme
With spirits free from Irish dream,
And hope to show you as they pass
Some charming girls as in a glass,
Where each may see just as she goes
Her lovely self from head to toes.

Immortal Gods, behold that girl—
Her ruby lips, her teeth of pearl!
Observe her smile—now hear her talk!
And oh, well mark that gliding walk!
Darling! Thou'rt all ethereal
With just enough of good material.
I swear 'tis true, I do not scoff,
One turn this way—By Jove!—she's off.

Until we chance to meet again,
My soul goes with you, bright Chataine.

But "Hold," my editor now cries,
"Make me a verse on ladies' eyes,
And ladies' looks and ladies' smiles,
And of their dress that most beguiles."

My dearest Sir, I say you this:
Of glowing Dame or budding Miss
I may, perhaps, descant in rhyme
Wanting in tune and out of time;
But when you bid me sing of clothes—
Ah well, *Cá c'est bien autre chose.*
This I say not as a railer
But truth to tell, I'm not a tailor.

TWILIGHT—SUNLIGHT—FLOWERS—WOMEN.

Sweet, indeed, is the twilight hour,
As all must own who've felt its power—
That hour so soft, so gently stealing
Around the soul, Love's thought revealing.

Of this have sung in dreamy mood
Poets ere Byron or Tom Hood.

But ah! Give me this noonday sun
With scenes as oft I've gazed upon.
A landscape here—there shady bowers
Where one might rest 'midst fragrant flowers;
Nor care, nor think, of aught beside,
The universe his blushing bride.
Flowers! I love you most in nature
But can't o'ercome your nomenclature.

And now for women—that is, ladies—
Ever our charmers! E'en in Hades

I could adore and worship you
As I do here, nor mind the rue.

Skies and flowers and women, all
Our best sensations you enthrall;
That is, we worship, though afar,
Each one his own ethereal star.
How bright, how beautiful, how true
To live forever here with you;
Leaving to creeds their full transmission
To heaven hereafter, or perdition.

But hold! I must not moralize,
Nor treat of things beyond our skies;
But leave unto each holy father
To damn or save us as he'd rather.
For me, enough that here I am
"*Ne sutor ultra crepidam.*"

A SKETCH.

THE REAL AND THE IDEAL.

"Divinely tall" and so divinely fair"
This "daughter of the gods" with golden hair
Is now no frenzy of the poet's eye—
She's here; in flesh and blood her I descry
As spurred and booted on she prances,
Casting broadcast her timid (?) glances.—
Here, O poet, your ideal I find
In ample habit and waist confined,
Well trimmed with laces, satins and so forth
With all the fripperies now put on by Worth.
Fringes and fripperies all combined
To improve for you the form of womankind.

O worthy Worth! How you make up the shape!
And whether short or tall, a nymph you make.
A nymph! Ye fools, hand-made for such as you
Whose souls are inane as her leathern shoe!

For me, for me, avaunt thou painted vision!
I've nought to give thee but my soul's derision—
Ah, yes, I have; though 'tis not wise nor witty,
I tender thee a true man's honest pity.

I turn me from this Fiction to the True,
I turn, my own ideal, I turn to you!
I turn to something that my sight won't grieve—
To something of the old Miltonian Eve.

Then grant me, Venus, Heavenly Queen of Love,
Thou who still reigneth from thy throne above;
Grant me, O Queen, that I may live to see
Some breathing woman as my soul sees thee.
Some form of Egypt or of classic Rome,
Some one with whom my restless heart's at home;
Some one, dear Goddess, I no more may leave,
Some one with less of Worth but more of Eve;
Some one like this, O Goddess, deign to give,
And I thy votary shall ever live;
Nor other fancy e'er my heart shall stir,
For kneeling at thy shrine I'll love but her.

A BIRTHDAY WISH.

Dear J——, to-day you're twenty-four!
May your years reach to four-score more
   And happiness abound!
And when, at length, the Master calls
You hence from earthly routs and balls,
   May you be worthy found!

And midst the pure and Heavenly host
Find, and rejoin, the Loved and Lost
   Whom we are mourning here!
And I, when my poor life is done,
And all my sins are cleansed and gone,
   May I, too, join you there!

TO HER.

> To her—a gentle one—
> Whom I have worshiped long
> I dedicate this song.

I love her, though she knows it not,
    For words of love I have not spoken;
But yet my soul has not forgot
    To send to her its truthful token.

Has sent it from mine eyes to hers
    Whilst seeing her waste on idiot lispers
The glances that are only Love's,
    When Love speaks in softest whispers.

I love her, though she knows it not,—
    Ah, yes, she does, for where's the woman
That ever yet the art forgot
    To read us first, we poor males human.

I love her gray blue eyes so bright,
    My soul flits lovingly about 'em,

The stars above show no such light,
    This world to me is dark without 'em.

I love her winsome honest smile
    Showing to me her teeth of pearl,
That all my sorrows could beguile,
    I do so love this gentle girl.

I love her quiet high-bred air,
    Her handsome hands, her shapely ankle,
Oh, I could gaze for ever there,
    Nor care nor grief my soul would rankle.

I love her lips—her lips I love,
    Those lips so chaste yet so enticing,
The saints would leave their thrones above
    Could they but touch them on alighting.

I love her—yes, ye gods, I do,
    And roundly swear by every sonnet
I worship her from hat to shoe,
    Yes, from her shoe up to her bonnet.

A HEALTH TO HER.

Byron would pledge the health of Moore,
    In water pure and clear—
A draught all fit for Friendship sure,
    When nothing better's near.

But I, who am no poet, nor
    Can boast me much of brain
Would pledge the girl that this is for
    In bumpers of champagne.

Here in our sanctum snug and trim,
    All selfish thoughts above,
Fill, sirs, your glasses to the brim
    I give—"The girl I love."

"What is her name? Pray who is she?
    Now, we'll have no excuse.
Where does she live? Now tell it me?
    I'm sure you won't refuse."

My friends, I will not give her name
   Though here I do not boast,
So if to you 'tis all the same
   We'll now drink deep my toast.

Here's to her azure eyes so bright,
   Here's to her modest carriage!
And here's to her by day and night,
   Both now and after marriage!

And here's to her with all my heart,
   For she could never pall it!
Here's to each artless artful art
   By which she can enthrall it!

And here's to her!—But let me see—
   Why this poetic feeling?
I know not if she cares for me
   Whilst unto her I'm kneeling.

TO MESDAMES S—— AND T——.

By sad sea waves and mountains grand
   They tell me you are now residing.
May wave and zephyr blend on strand
   To bring you joy whilst there abiding.

And may each drive or ride or walk
   By mountain side or calm seashore,
Be such as in the soul's mute talk
   Bring mem'ries sweet for evermore.

This much from one who ne'er beguiles,
   Whose nature's cold as it may be;
Whose heart is proof 'gainst woman's wiles,
   But not, against her sympathy.

Sweet sympathy — that precious gift!
   To your dear sex seems to be given
To strengthen man — his hopes to lift,
   And bring him back when lost to Heaven.

For, dreaming wearily of things,
    Dead to this world and all its strife,
Your visit still in my soul rings
    And leads me back again to life.

Dear ladies, this you freely gave —
    Your gentle nature's sympathy ;
When I lay soulless as the wave
    That frets and dies on yonder sea.

Then may I send in simple verse
    Greetings to you from this sick-bed,
In words not either wise nor terse —
    Straight from the heart, not from the head.

SAN FRANCISCO, June 16, 1888.

A STAVE FOR IRELAND.

Sing, O my muse!
You can't refuse
To give one stave for Ireland;
For there amidst her streams and brooks,
Her mountains high and pleasant nooks,
We drew our thoughts out Nature's books
Of Love and Truth and Ireland.

In times gone by
'Neath that soft sky,
We dreamed of Love and Ireland;
And now though far from her we roam,
She's still to us our own heart's home,
The dearest spot beneath God's dome —
Our own, our native Ireland.

There first we sung
When days were young
Of Love and Truth and Ireland;

And here to-night, though somewhat old,
With heart and spirits growing cold,
We'd draw one thought from ancient mould
    Of Love and Truth and Ireland.

    Then let us sing,
    And try to bring
  One thought to-night for Ireland.
It is the hope her sons may be
United all fraternally—
That is the thought to pledge with me
    For Love and Truth and Ireland.

    And on that day
    O'er land and bay
  In every home in Ireland,
Peace and Contentment full shall reign
And Justice rule o'er land and main,
Whilst from each hearth comes one refrain
    For Love and Truth and Ireland.

ODE OF THANKSGIVING.

Written at Request of a Catholic Lady, a Member of St. Mary's Cathedral.

Father of all, enthroned on high,
Lord of the sea and earth and sky,
We tender Thee a joyful cry
    On this auspicious day;
For Thou has brought from o'er the main,
Our Bishop safely home again,
For life, with us, here to remain
    And strengthened for the fray.

O Lord, Thy people's thanks receive,
For all their needs Thou dost relieve,
Nor let those for Thy favors grieve
    Who place their trust in Thee,—
Let us, O Lord, Thy mercies praise;
With love and truth our hearts now raise,
That on Thy presence we may gaze
    In all humility.

And now, your Grace, we welcome you
From Tiber old and Danube blue,
And thank our God with hearts still true
    We have you here at home.
Be yours, my lord, our souls to guide;
Remain, kind Guardian, at our side;
Be ours, from you, not once to glide
    Nor with false teachers roam.

And when, at last, our race is run,
And eyes shall close on earthly sun,
May He, to us, then say, "Well done";
    And, in the realms above,
May we behold thee, mitered there!
Prince, of our Church, in heaven's own sphere
Our spirits blended everywhere
    In God's own link of love.

A MONODY:

WITH REGRETFUL REFERENCE TO THE DEATH OF A DEAR FRIEND.

O muse of mine, must we again
So soon take up a mournful strain,
And grief, for aye, be our refrain
   Whilst lingering here below?
If this be so, then let us bend
Our hearts, our souls, unto the end
That He to us may also send
   Strength to accept each blow.

O Lord, Thou, in Thy wisdom, hast
From me estranged in the past
Those I have loved, and this the last
   Thou hast now also taken.
Thy will, O Lord, on earth be done
From rising unto setting sun,
And when life's petty battle's won
   Let me not be forsaken;

But in Thy realms, where heart meets heart,
Cemented never more to part,
'Midst Mankind from Creation's start
   Of every creed and clime
May I, O God, in mercy find
Those I have sought in soul and mind
Our intercourse there unconfined,
   Blended unto all time.

San Francisco,
   April 10, 1889.

AN INTROSPECTIVE MUSING.

I look within, and there I see
Thoughts madly struggling to be free
With which I am in sympathy;
    But yet, I with Montaigne
Do think that if inside my hand
All human truths I could command,
I'd better give it to the brand
    Than open it amain.

And, so I think and thus I dream
That most things are not what they seem,
Nor dare we let the sunlight beam
    Upon some thoughts of ours;
For this our world is still but young
And some things must be left unsung,
Although the withers may be wrung
    While Darkness overpowers.

Yes, Frenchman wise, you were quite right
In courting not an earthy fight
Where all is wrong that is not might;
    As it so stands to-day
In every land beneath the sun
Where nought is lost, but all is won
By those who've got the mightiest gun
    And bring it into play.

Then, dreams of mine, we'll dream no more,
Or if we do, 't is not before
We study well the cannon's bore
    And know how it will suit us;
And then in cause of human kind
We'll battle both with gun and mind,
Confronting tyrants who shall find
    They cannot thus refute us.

So, thoughts of mine, back to your caves,
Nor surge you thus in maddening waves,
But rest you still as sleeping babes
    Until your time shall come;

Then, nor with weak nor tuneless tongue,
The Good and Wise and Brave among,
Speak you the truth to old and young
With voice of loudest drum.

TO "A."

(IN REPLY TO HER REQUEST.)

My dearest girl, you ask of me
To write one verse on "Vanity."
If I comply, then let us see
    What may in truth be said.
That vanity is sinful doth
Go without saying, and of sloth
Or indolence is born, or both—
    My heart thinks with my head.

Dear little girl, if e'er you feel
Your gentle soul toward it steal
Curb it right then for your own weal
    Nor place therein your trust,
For vanity, when it begins,
Forerunner is of other sins
And man's respect it never wins
    But rather his disgust.

Be never vain, but be thou *proud!*
In solitude or midst the crowd
Let conscience ever speak aloud,
    And God will do the rest;
Bearing thee with humility
That all may see thee as He'd see,
And He will kindly foster thee
    And guide thee for the best.

Be ever truthful, never vain!
So on your soul shall be no stain,
And blessings on you He will rain
    Unto the end of life;
Raise your heart ever up to Him,
Nor be the slave of passion's whim;
And youth's deep cup full to the brim
    With gladness shall be rife.

This, little girl, is what I'd say
From my retreat across the bay,
Here, dreaming on this Holy day,
    Far from the city's throng.

So wishing you a happy year
With heart and conscience ever clear,
And praying He may hold you dear,
    I send my friendly song.

SAUCELITO,
  Palm Sunday, '89.

LE JOUR DE L'AN.

IS IT A DREAM?

Written for the Knights of St. Patrick, and recited at their banquet on the 17th of March, 1886.

This day brings us glorious weather,
    Clouds have vanished, skies are clear,
For now we stand on native heather
    On this *our* one day of the year.

Nor sects nor creeds to-day shall blind us,
    Except it be the creed of love;
"Thus may the world forever find us,"
    Is Erin's prayer to heaven above.

Brethren all to-day united,
    By St. Patrick from above;
Each content, there's no one slighted,
    All are linked in bonds of love.

To-day there's neither Boyne nor Shannon
    Liffy, nor yet old rebel Lee;

Nor siege of Derry, nor Dungannon;
  Ribbon, nor Orange can I see.

Orange and Green are one forever;
  Sworn to one country and one cause,
They to be disunited never
  For now we have Home Rule—Home Laws!

To-day we stand one band of brothers,
  Doing to all as all require—
True to our ourselves, friendly to others,—
  A spectacle the gods inspire.

To-day, one only thought is spoken,
  As brother clasps a brother's hand;
Each one wearing Ireland's token,—
  The Shamrock of our Native Land.

Other lands may have their flowers,
  Rose or Thistle, as they may;
But thou, dear emblem, still art ours
  To bring us close on Patrick's Day.

Then here's to thee our own lov'd Erin!
  Here's to each Irish heart so true
That near or far this day is wearing
  The shamrock green for love of you!

Confusion then to traitors all,
  That e'er in thought or word or deed
Have sought to compass Ireland's fall,
  Or would deny her in her need!

Such thoughts avaunt! Here is no treason,
  That fatal curse has pass'd away.
We're loyal men with right and reason,
  In Friendship met on Patrick's Day.

Then fill the bowl, each Irish brother,
  This is a day of joy I deem.
—Let's drown the Shamrock,— now another!
  Is this all *real*, or do I dream?

This is no dream! I see before me!
  My country's woes are past and dead.

This is no phrenzy that comes o'er me,
　I only see some years ahead.

Then pledge we fresh each Irish brother,
　Our day of joy has come 'twould seem.
Let's drown the Shamrock — now one other!
　We'll make this real — and not a dream.

PEN PORTRAITS.

Archbishop Riordan.

Tall and erect alone he stands,
This chosen chief of chosen bands
From varied climes and far-off lands,
    With power on his face;
From altar or from pulpit he
Discourses with simplicity,
With eloquence—with dignity—
    My friends, behold his Grace.

The Vicar-General, Father Prendergast.

With native ease and subtle grace,
With intellect that all can trace
In every line upon his face,
    With kind yet searching ken,
True scholar; yet, without pretense;
Giving advice without offense,
As priest or man in truest sense—
    This is good Father "Pren."

The Chancellor, Father Montgomery.

> Nervous and quick in act and thought,
> Yet never seeming overwrought,
> Spontaneous wisdom never sought
> 	Nor offered charily.
> Urbane and scholarly you'll find
> This restless man with quiet mind;
> Calm centre of a whirling wind —
> 	Our Père Montgomery.

A SERENADE.

Wake! Lady mine, the moon is beaming
    And stars above now dimly shine,
Whilst here am I, so lonely, dreaming
    Ever of thee, O lady mine!

Rise! Lady mine, the heavens greet thee,
    Trembling high in the midnight hue,
Whilst my fond heart shall joyful meet thee,
    Ever mine own, both fond and true!

Come forth, come forth! my craving heart's love,
    Come forth and view this night so clear!
Come forth, come forth! my thirsting soul's love,
    Cease all doubting, 'tis I am here.

Come forth, come forth! now O mine only love,
    Come forth and show the stars their queen!
Come forth, come forth! now O mine only love,
    To-night we'll wander far unseen.

To-night we'll roam where sleeping flowerlets,
    love,
Lead us a-straying with their perfume sweet,
And lingering lost in their leafy bowerlets, love,
    We'll list in silence to our own hearts beat.

HEALTH TO SUE.

Once on a time a poet grand,
Awhile his boat was on the strand,
    His barque upon the sea,
Could take a stoup of water cool,
(Would I could drink from out that pool
    Though not so deep as he.)

That pool has long since dried and gone,
And we are left to plod alone
    As weakly mortals may;
So I must take a stronger drink,
And let my deep aversion sink
    Upon this festal day.

Then give me rich and glowing wine,
And let me see your bright eyes shine
    As ne'er they shone before;
And I shall call upon the muse.
(Slow jade, she will not now refuse
    But answer as of yore.)

In vain, alas, in vain I call,
There is not here within this hall
    To whom my muse will cater.
For she is a capricious elf
And flies betimes e'en from myself,
    And so do not berate her.

But there is one—were she now here—
To whom the muse would warble clear
    In notes of true devotion;
Then we would canter right along,
And breathe our music into song
    Of which you have no notion.

Still yet, old nag, now ere we part—
You're crusty though not ill of heart—
    This once you won't refuse?
Come! let us show these people we
Are lacking not in courtesy
    Though cat'ring to the muse.

'Tis well! my friends, the muse relents.
If wrongs she here has said repents,
    And this is her adieu.
Come drain your glasses right away,
And damned in Beauty's eyes be they
    Who drink not unto Sue!

BACCHANALIAN.

Set me a stoup of the red, red wine!
The glowing, gleaming, red, red wine!
And you, my girl, with the face divine,
Now pledge me deep in the red, red wine!
    The glowing, gleaming, red, red wine!
    The drowsy, dreaming, red, red wine!

Your lips, my fair, were made for mine;
Deep in your eyes love's longings shine;
Around my soul your raptures twine!
Come, pledge again in the red, red wine!
    This rosy, reeking, red, red wine!
    This shimmering, shining, red, red wine!

We'll laugh and quaff till daylight's shine,
(Nor balk that crafty Boy's design),
And memory, grief, and all repine
Are drowned deep, deep, in the guilty wine!
    The maddening, murderous, red, red wine!
    The gory, guilty, red, red wine!

A RECOLLECTION OF THE YOSEMITE.

O, that moonlight and that valley!
    Before me them I see!
O, that moonlight and that valley!
    Of the Yosemite!

And, oh, to me that dearest time
    When at her feet I lay!
Would I could here produce in rhyme
    All that I thought that day!

The moon creeps o'er the mountain
    Leaving one-half in shade,
The rippling of the fountain
    Blends with the loud cascade.

And the night winds sighing round us
    And earth's great dome above,
And the kindly eyes that found us
    Lost in our dream of love.

And the words that were unspoken
　And thoughts left unexpressed,
And the promises unbroken
　That never were confessed.

And the silence and the parting
　As there we said "good night,"
And the murmuring and the starting
　Of one good friend's affright.

And since that night, the years have gone —
　Aye, I believe, a score.
Of all that throng I see not one
　Nor may for evermore.

The memory of that lovely night
　And of its moonlight clear
In my fond soul shall e'er be bright
　With all that I hold dear.

A VALENTINE.

From St. Valentine's Court I hail afar!
    Kentucky late was my home,
And guided now by Love's own star
    On a mission of Love I roam.

I hail from a Land of Southern sun;
    I've travel'd many a mile;
O'er mountains and gorges wild I've come
    To gather from thee—*one smile.*

I have left behind me a glowing land—
    Its softest and brightest of skies
To me was a desert, cold and bland,
    For it lacked the light of your eyes.

I have said adieu to its flowers so fair;
    To its waters where sunbeams dance,
I reach this city's dusty glare
    To crave from thee—*one glance!*

I 've heard of your beauty. It warmed my heart;
   I 've heard of it many a time;
I 've *read* of it often,—nay do not start,
   I 've read it in very poor rhyme!

I am come, I knock at your true heart's gate,
   . I 'm come without fear or sin;
Oh, say not I 'm tardy; say not too late,
   But bid me to hasten in.

I enter; I bless you; I lie at your feet;
   Forgetting each weary mile,
As you take me up with a welcome sweet
   And yield what I asked—one smile!

That winsome smile! To me now given
   Illumines a heart all true;
And nestles there as a beam from Heaven
   Sent into a soul through you.

You look me over. Oh, read me once more!
   You ponder. Is it only a chance?

You put me away, but 't is not before
   You have giv'n what I crav'd—one glance!

That one fleeting glance! O, paper cold,
   Think not it can stay with thee!
No, no, in the ways of some fairy bold,
   It hastens to stay with me.

That smile and glance in my life shall live
   So long as the bright stars shine.
My love and my rhyme, sweet girl, forgive
   I am only a valentine.

MUSING.

Valentine's Day has come and gone,
And I've writ missives more than one
    To suit each fair one's notion;
But one dear girl o'er all I've seen
Whose quiet grace and noble mien
    Absorb my heart's devotion.

And yet to her I have not writ,
Nor sent of token e'er a bit
    That in the least might move her;
For she has gold whilst none have I,
And so in silence must I sigh,
    Nor speak how much I love her.

Let Fate or Chance this lot reverse,
Then love's own story I'll rehearse
    And tell her, O how boldly,
All that this heart of mine has felt
Since first mine eyes upon her dwelt,
    Though trying to look coldly.

Shall I now seek me other eyes
And gaze in them with feigned surprise,
    To try me to forget her?
'T were all in vain, each word and look
Of hers are stamp'd in my life's book,
    And were since first I met her.

I can't bring back a by-gone age
When pelfless wight might act the page—
    Such ways no longer suit us;
So I shall do as others do,
And since I can't wed her, I'll woo
    And worship thee, O Plutus!

Then, god of riches, grant thou me
Some trifle of the wealth I see
    Thou show'rst so on asses,
That I may speak outside of song,
And love and cherish my life long
    This fairest of fair lassies.

A CHRISTMAS CAROL.

O, Christmas bells loud ring,
And unto my soul bring
Thoughts that I would sing,
    In not unworthy rhyme!
For on this day was born
Of wealth and pomp though shorn
In stable all forlorn
    Peace unto all time.

For ages long before
The weight of crime man bore,
Nor could he clear the score
    Of mortal sins anent him;
But on this blessed day
Unto Time's distant sway
O'er every land and bay
    Is forgiveness sent him.

Then, O, you Christians all
Of station low or tall
In every home, though small,
    Your enmities now cease.
And let a kindly love
Thus sanctioned from above
In peaceful spirit rove
    From Heav'n-born Babe of Peace.

A PARK CAROL:

LINES SUGGESTED UPON READING ARCHBISHOP RIORDAN'S PROPOSITION OF RAISING ONE HUNDRED THOUSAND DOLLARS FOR PARK IMPROVEMENTS AND TO GIVE WORK TO THE NEEDY UNEMPLOYED.

Now, purse-proud city by the sea,
A song of praise I sing to thee,
    And to thy true men all
Who've cast aside turmoils and broils,
And filthy lust for filthy spoils
    To hear the laborers' call.

And you, Archbishop, bold and grand,
Who now would lead this noble band—
    My homage at thy door,—
For thou dost well the Master's will—
His kind behests thou dost fulfill
    In caring for His poor.

And I have crossed through "Golden Gate,"
By dawn's soft light and evening late,
    Nor lark, thrush, linnet found,—
But each wee bird that I met there
Twittered thy praises everywhere
    From perches near the ground.

Go on, good Bishop, in thy way
Nor trouble what false men may say.
    Go, ramble, through the Park,
And there the flowers shall smile on you
And trees and ferns give welcome, too—
    Of Nature's love a mark.

SAN FRANCISCO,
    March 6, 1890.

NOTES TO IRISH RECOLLECTIONS.

"Hooker" is a vessel with one mast, of from twenty to eighty tons burden, and is manned by a crew of two. The "Nanny's" capacity was about fifty tons. She usually made monthly return trips from Roundstone, in Connemarra, to Galway, the capital of Connaught, a distance of forty miles, and was owned and sailed by Martin Toole, assisted by the "Commodore," as he was called, an excellent seaman, though deaf as a post. It has been the good fortune of the writer to have had many a sail in the hooker along that bold Coast; and, although he has since seen much of this world, he can still look back to those innocent recreations with pleasurable feelings, and can honestly state that in all his wanderings he has seen no marine scenes to equal those which then met his youthful gaze.

"Errisbeg" is the name of a mountain in the neighborhood of Roundstone, in the County of Galway. It is the most forward of the range on that coast, and from its isolation and position appeals to the imagination as the advanced guard or picket on duty of the hoary ramparts behind it, protecting old Ireland from an invasion of the Atlantic. Sir Walter Scott said the finest view in Ireland was from Torc mountain in Killarney. No doubt the view from Torc is very beautiful. But had the great novelist stood on the summit of Errisbeg, I do not think he would yield the palm to Torc quite so readily; for standing on Errisbeg magnificent views present themselves on all sides. On his right he would see a vast plain intersected with many lakes, dotted with small islands, stretching away towards Clifden, the capital of Connemarra. On his left the island of Ennislaken (almost at his feet), the bay of Roundstone and Moyross with its strongly indented coasts; in front of him the magnificent Atlantic in its billowy undulations rolling off to this great Republic; while at his back lie the "Twelve Pens," lazily sleeping in their Alpine repose. The writer, though not born there, spent years of early childhood and boyhood in that neighborhood, and on leaving Ireland called to have a farewell look at the old hill. He spent the day with his kind, hospitable friend, Father James. They had an early four o'clock dinner in his cosy cottage at the foot of Letterdiffe, after which they strolled up towards "Errisbeg." Their parting was as described.

IRISH RECOLLECTIONS.

Martin Toole.

What though he's but a boatman—
   An honest man is he
As ever sailed afloat, man,
   On calm or stormy sea.

And his good ship the "Nanny"
   Or hooker I should say,
He plies so bold and canny
   Upon old Galway's bay.

It's many a pleasant sailing
   We've had along that shore,
With none to hear our railing
   But the deaf old Commodore.

What if of pigs and other stock
   He often had a cargo—
Think you his humor it did block
   Or cause the least embargo?

No, for the pigs and ladies
    He did the best he could,
As also for the babies
    Who were not "in the wood."

Oft on the wild rude ocean
    A-tossing on the deep,
Each wave with huge commotion
    Kept rocking them from sleep.

Since then I've had some sailing
    With sail full to the rim,
But not the pleasant railing
    That I have had with him.

And, if I now sing this boatman
    Think not the worse of me,
I've said he was as true a man
    As sails upon the sea.

And sure in this, as other things,
    No matter how it turns,

Or how the trump of fame now rings,
   I think wi' Bobby Burns.

I think with Scotland's poet tramp
   In lines both terse and pat,
"The rank is but the guinea's stamp,"
   The head is not the hat.

Here's to you, jolly boatman,
   One of the olden school—
With you I'd be afloat, man—
   Here's to you, Martin Toole.

Father James.

The eve was calm, all earth lay still,
We sat beneath Errisbeg hill—
That ancient hill that o'er the strand
Towers to Olympus, lone and grand;
Proud and erect alone it stands,
An ancient guard o'er ancient lands;
Holding in check Atlantic's waves,
It sends them backward to their caves.

O, dear old hill, to my fond youth
How fair you seemed, and yet, in sooth,
Seeing earth's mountains grand and tall
Thou art still dearest of them all!
My memory backward hurries now,
Ere care was written on my brow,
Those happy days so long gone by
When sporting like each butterfly
That up and down thy old side gleamed
And dancing as the bright sun beamed—

When I as bright and pure as they
Could revel in the full noon day,
Nor thought nor dreamt that one blast might
Plunge my bright day to darkest night.

Beneath this hill there sat that night
As loath to leave while waning light
Sufficed for conversation slight;—
Two friends who talked how 'neath the sun
This world has often been undone
By tricks of knaves or woman's fun;
Of Ireland's wrongs if e'er they'd right
By "moral force" or battle's might.

One of these two, a layman, was
Depressed this night with grievous cause;
For he was leaving sad and lone
The place which long had been his home
To wander forth strange scenes to meet,
And ne'er perchance his own land greet—
That land to him the first on earth—
Home of his heart—land of his birth!

The other, priest of that old faith
Which time nor chains nor whilom death
Could shake from out that country's breath,
One of those guides in whom you scan
The pious priest and honest man.

Nor beads nor gown this eve behold,
But by the light of burnished gold
The sun is shedding o'er the mountain,
Ere he forsakes each dale and fountain
To play the part of love's recluse—
Hid from all eyes except the muse;
And in soft dreams Thetis beside
Forget our world with his ocean bride,—
And by the light of one bright star
That now is coming from afar,
Instead of rosary might be seen
A tiny flask of clear poteen—
Spirit so pure to see it now
The Turk might drink, nor break his vow.

"I pledge you true," the good priest said,
As swift his heart flew to his head.
"I pledge you true," 'twas urged with grief,
"Take it, my friend, 'twill give relief.
Now once again, and then good-night—
God bless you, may your days be bright."

And since that night I've wandered far
On ocean life, a drifting spar,
Now sometimes up and sometimes down,
Sometimes a smile, again a frown,
As if my life had been but made
A plaything for the Fickle Jade.
Hopes bright and dark mayhap betimes,
As I would show in some weak rhymes,
Have chased each other o'er my soul
Nor yet have found a resting goal.
As light and shadow may be seen
Flitting across a village green,
Or coming down the steepest hill
To seek for refuge in a rill;

Anon to leave the gentle river
Again to chase each other ever.—
Such is our life—such most men are
Each but the plaything of his star.

For me, where'er my lot be cast,
In summer's calm or winter's blast,
Remember thee? Aye, to the last!
Whilst yet to Love or Friendship's flames
My heart may throb, dear Father James,
Whate'er may come to sooth or fret
That land and thee I'll ne'er forget.

But ah, my pen, hold on, no more!
For thou, dear friend, art gone before—
Gone to those Realms where we are taught
Honor and Truth need not be sought—
Gone in thy prime *sans* earthly dross,
Whilst I am left to mourn thy loss.
Left alone in this world of sin,
One only thought still left therein,—
The hope the dream to meet again
Thy spirit pure, amen, amen!

www.ingramcontent.com/pod-product-compliance
Lightning Source LLC
Chambersburg PA
CBHW031403160426
43196CB00007B/884